Burlesques

ON THE SECRET BOOK OF JOHN

Egon H. E. Lass

FUTURECYCLE PRESS
www.futurecycle.org

Cover artwork, a composite of images and concepts in the public domain by Diane Kistner; cover and interior book design by Diane Kistner; Palatino text and titling, Zapfino "Burlesques"

Library of Congress Control Number: 2018932727

Copyright © 2018 Egon H. E. Lass
All Rights Reserved

Published by FutureCycle Press
Athens, Georgia, USA

ISBN 978-1-942371-72-4

For Patty, Craig, and Anna

The Secret Book of John is part of a number of Codices that were found in 1945 near the city of Nag Hammadi, Egypt. It dates to about 150 CE and is a Gnostic book, containing among other things a description of the creation of Adam. This was accomplished by a throng of 74 angels, each creating a small part of the whole.

THE CREATION OF ADAM

1. The Head
2. The Skull
3. The Brain
4. The Right Eye
5. The Left Eye
6. The Right Ear
7. The Left Ear
8. The Nose
9. The Lips
10. The Teeth
11. The Molars
12. The Tonsils
13. The Uvula
14. The Neck
15. The Vertebrae
16. The Throat
17. The Right Shoulder
18. The Left Shoulder
19. The Right Elbow
20. The Left Elbow
21. The Right Underarm
22. The Left Underarm
23. The Right Hand
24. The Left Hand
25. The Fingers of the Right Hand
26. The Fingers of the Left Hand
27. The Fingernails
28. The Right Breast
29. The Left Breast
30. The Right Shoulder Joint
31. The Left Shoulder Joint
32. The Belly
33. The Navel
34. The Abdomen
35. The Right Ribs
36. The Left Ribs
37. The Right Hip

38. The Left Hip
39. The Marrow
40. The Bones
41. The Stomach
42. The Heart
43. The Lungs
44. The Liver
45. The Spleen
46. The Intestines
47. The Kidneys
48. The Sinews
49. The Backbone
50. The Veins
51. The Arteries
52. The Breath in All the Limbs
53. All the Flesh
54. The Right Buttock
55. The Left Buttock
56. The Penis
57. The Testicles
58. The Genitals
59. The Right Thigh
60. The Left Thigh
61. The Muscles of the Right Leg
62. The Muscles of the Left Leg
63. The Right Leg
64. The Left Leg
65. The Right Shin
66. The Left Shin
67. The Right Ankle
68. The Left Ankle
69. The Right Foot
70. The Toes of the Right Foot
71. The Left Foot
72. The Toes of the Left Foot
73. The Toenails
74. …

Notes

The first angel, who is Raphao, began by creating the head

1. The Head

This will be the greatest head ever made!
The owner will use it to shape
A universe of judgments. Whom
Did they call to take responsibility?
Raphao, the first among equals,
Archangel extraordinaire at your service!
I swept through the galaxy,
Gathering stardust as I proceeded.
Foremost the eyes to perceive,
Nostrils to smell, a tongue to savor,
A mouth for the fruit and for the kiss,
Two ears to perceive music,
Or endearments whispered by foolish
Lovers suffering from self-inflicted
Imbecility! In the midst of it all, a brain,
The most refined material ever designed!
Climbing into itself, climbing back out, renewing itself
In every permutation, sinking to the lowest cesspools,
Brawling its way back to the surface,
Passing on traditions and wisdoms,
Tinkering at impossible devices
In the quest for a smooth existence,
Understanding all known things,
Wallowing in lunacy while being supreme
In wisdom, entangled in opposites
While searching for truth,
Conforming in a million ways
To the conventions of humanity,
While being radically inclined
To blow the whole thing to shreds,
Honing extravagance to a fine skill,
Doing the same with modesty.
The whole creation built
Of synthetics, the acquired

Abilities, synthetic as the edifice
That misguided hands will assemble.
Self-awareness will be synthetic
And perpetually amused by all
Of its own naïve expectations.

Abron created the skull

2. The Skull

Patron saint of all pirates,
Skull over crossed bones,
The Almighty thought it fitting
To appoint me maker of the skull.
May my skullduggery
Not be expiated on Golgotha.
May my frontal eminence
Not be humbled to the parietal,
Nor my mendosa be mendacious!
Día de los Muertos! Is this Jolly Roger
Meant to make me mindful
Of my mortal mortality?
Sutura your *annulus!*
I have no need to be reminded!
Dependably, every day at 6:30 p.m.,
I remind myself that I am the angel
Abron! Let me tell you, madam,
It was nothing, really. I took my rapier
And brandished it in wild gesticulations,
Like Zorro in rage, whittling the shape
From the deep *Tohu-va-Vohu,*
Thrusting out the eye-holes,
Sculpting a triangular hollow
For the nose, enormously hooked.
The lackey, Amen, fitted the teeth
After I had pruned the hubs.
Puck, puck, puck, they flew in,

As fast as hobnails shot from a gun.
And so, huh, well, what do you want?
It was a frame on which to hang
Fleshy faces, tender and refined, such
As yours, madam, mighty and ponderous;
Such as mine, trifling, piddling, small-bore,
And generally imbecilic, as seen
In most exemplars. Don't blame me—
I made only the canvas,
Not what later artists chose to dab on it.
The dutiful sphincters of all the priests
Forgot to clench at the moment of truth;
The violins sent all of their guts
Into a *Magnificat interruptus!*

Meniggesstroeth created the brain

3. The Brain

Intelligence is something
That humans take the trouble developing.
The Adam in your workshop, Meniggesstroeth,
Has been hallucinating
At the installation of every component.
Keep the tigers hidden in the murk of Deep-Spine Six.
How is your creature supposed to keep track
Of its electrons, if they vanish on one side
Of a synapse, and reappear pitter-pattering
In custody? You engineered a billionfold
Tunneling effect every time there is thought
Of scratching a nose or crotch?
The donated zona incerta is inerta like a rock
Of iron ore. Has there ever been life in it?
Where are the consummatory consummations?
You ran out an ulcer on the tongue,
A spinning compass in the cup,
An epileptic seizure in the movement of its prime,

A block throughout its natural establishment.
Get the iron stoker moving,
Before it melts like a gummy bear
In the mouth of your graven image.
Look at the gash of wounds he will have to
Endure. Somewhere there must be
A hiding place for the supernatural.
There must be a possibility
For miracles, miraculous healings
Of the unhealable. There must be
Prototypes and symbols, elusive proof
That you exist, and that it was you
Who did all this, created the silhouette
Of being, created the footprints
That come from nothing and lead nowhere.
Blind faith in every fairy tale
That survives more than a century,
Heedless pigheadedness willing to fight
To the death in defense of imbecilic
Proclamations, which are in every way
As real as any physical brain.

Asterechme created the right eye

4. The Right Eye

There is no light perception
In any of the eyes.
The right one, circle-sided in quadrature,
Glazes over too many times a day,
Because there is no suffering
Of fools and villains.
No more blinking at the spry.
There is some color this eye keeps seeing.
Asterechme concludes
It was created by jealousy,
A soul of skin, black, yellow, red, white,

But to the right eye,
Something mixed, nothing pure,
Hybrid, vigor, mingling,
Because the cells are prancing,
The DNA is leaping to snap it up,
And there is no right eye
Sending messages to the wrong head,
That will ever carry the day in obstruction.
May a macular degeneration bite your bottom.
Through dry eye syndrome,
This eye is offended at everything it sees
Pared down, peed on, mauled
By goons supposedly of its own species.
They are giving this right eye red-eye,
Like a riverboat wheel
Plowing through garbage water.
Why is it swimming in rivers of bone?
How are the crimes it has committed
More atrocious than the daily murders
In this demented city?
If there is a judgment to be made,
Let the judge wear punk clothing
And be a flamboyant transvestite,
And as for those suffering from
Bigoted myopathy, the cheapest pair of glasses
Can be found for them,
Cheaper than any melted civilization.

Thaspomocha created the left eye

5. The Left Eye

Battling with demons,
He got stuck in his left eye
With a skewer normally used
For puncturing a gut full of regurgitation,
Forcing a blank on a blink,

Flavored fillet of virago.
And have you heard of all-body weeping?
What are the possibilities,
The likelihoods for the creation
Of a left eye, concocted by someone like
Thaspomocha, the geek in the class?
Fade into the Soviet laboratories where,
Opening the lids of her left eye,
She looked down the corridor,
Her pupil dilated like a growing black hole,
Saw the egg suspended,
Proceeded to separate the yellow from the white,
Surrounding witnesses drawing in breath,
Until the yellow was on the left,
The white on the right, and she
Two kilograms lighter in weight.
Does the moon really have a bald eye?
Is this a seesaw? One eye up, the other down?
Too many imps with too much power.
Does the right eye get jealous
Of the left? Does the left refuse to duel,
Or do you wind up cross-eyed?
I'm in love with you,
Said the ophthalmologist to the slit lamp.
The slit lamp kept blinking,
Causing the eye to be inflamed and bloodshot
Weeks after the final once-over.

Yeronumos created the right ear

6. The Right Ear

Two termini east and west
Of the temples, a terrain purported
To be gleefully wicked.
The otolith in the right inner ear
 Challenging the designer, Yeronumos (Geronimo?),

Lurching in that direction,
Lunging through a window pane
And onto the sidewalk, as if
Shot from a cannon. Draw!
Says someone, but owing to the lack
Of balance, a finger gets stuck in the belt,
Thus loosening the britches,
Falling down around the ankles,
And the six-shooter flies off to the right
Into the wooden tub used for washing
Madam Tinnitus's laundry.
For the meta-ear sounds have been
Morphing toward the uncultured,
People cursing on busses and trains,
In front of parent-carrying babies,
The Babel babble coming out of bistros
And swimming pools would render
A deaf-mute sternly cajoled.
My right ear dominates in favor reception.
It may discriminate between
Assault phonemes and timbres of nuisance,
The pitch of aspiring dimwits,
The clash of perspiring hoodlums.
Should it be closed to pleading,
Or moans of the dying, and much prefer
Voices of vacuous senators rocking
In luxurious yachts on Caribbean waters?
And there we were,
In frigid land, the wind
Snapping at us from the right,
And plunging further into the depth of the auditory canal,
With sharp tongues of hoarfrost,
All our extrasensory elocution unable
To convince him
That an ear is no vagina.

Bissoum created the left ear

7. The Left Ear

Speak to me from the right,
Sing sweetly to me from the left.
Bissoum, there is a French cast
To thy gleaming eye, and where
Have we met before in the spectral ambit?
Was it the artificial left
That grew on the backside of a mouse?
The naked Vacanti, not your favorite streamlined
Mongoose. We are practiced exultantly
In not hearing, even through mice in the buff.
Alright! I'm ready to confess!
Sure that my neighbor's hairpins
Are antennae transmitting top-secret messages
To spaceships out there, just beyond sight,
That the oak on the front lawn is an alien transplant.
It whispered to me, whispered strange things
In the night, all brought to you compliments of the left ear.
What's that you say? Brackets. Fracturing brackets,
Fracturing ridges! Will ye have a toffee?
No, no! Of course! No, no! Of course!
A most succulent…a most succulent…ridges!
Did Ariel enchant my ear? Did my face
Turn toffee and melt into a bassoon?
Vibration shining through membrane,
Not ear enough for Bach, not large enough
To embrace the Almighty, all hearing but most humbled,
There is no aural equipment to embrace humility.
We must hear like the deaf, a silence
Beyond vindication, a sound beyond cosmic collision.
Are the eyes, contemplating allure, able
To give more pleasure than the ears?
He knew the call of goats spread
All over valley and mountain,

He knew the call of dogs
Running over desert sand,
The call of jackals, frogs, donkeys;
Almost couldn't stand the noise,
The noise of the women arguing
Over who would do to him
What the sirens did to Odysseus.

Akioreim created the nose

8. The Nose

Rare the man could sniff out a ripe banana
From a green one.
Could his name be Cyrano,
Akioreim? Why not like dogs?
Too perfect for a creature designed
To be imperfect and needy,
His lack filled by companions?
The joy of walking seaward,
Land changing to a dunescape,
Sharp smell of nets
Strung out along the sandy road,
Smokehouses and racks of drying fish
Next to slate-roofed cottages.
The ocean beckoning with a salty wind,
Seductive curve of a schooner's bow,
Visceral adolescent longing for the high seas,
There is no other smell,
Until you've met your first woman,
Inhaled lavender,
Inhaled her breath and dark hair,
Collected dark seeds from her lips,
Your body her field, sometimes a meadow
In which to roll or rest in tall grass,
To plow with palms and fingernails
Among the scents of autumn, sowing fruits,

Irrigating wild flowers, digging deeply down
For ores of aromatized flesh,
Going through beauty staggers,
Lip frenzies, nose rages, in the ditch
Looking for yesterday's alimentary curses.
Snuffboxes not royally appointed
Fell on the rug next to our buckled shoes.
Your insufflation lacks the proper commitment,
Hits fail to be swift, and the flavor has no delivery,
Sir! Train your nose on camphor and cinnamon.
Your beaked sniffer is like a southern red velvet cake,
Too slathered with cream. Outhouses and pigsties,
Without the benefit of lime. If it wasn't me,
And it wasn't you, then why is my nose
Dispatching these messages of terror?

Banen-Ephroum created the lips

9. The Lips

Father of all mouth fetishes,
Banen-Ephroum, exit of the soul,
What a variable face-place!
Sneer of the emperors, whine of the guilty,
World kiss and damnation,
Utterance of curse and poem,
Union of opposites in pinnacle embrace,
Rouge administered and brought to bear
Beyond the natural borders,
Because we know what hypnotizes,
What draws the blue-collar hand
To his Machiavellian doom.
Transplanted to infinite Warhol images,
If you don't know how to use them
Aerodynamically, just pucker up and blow.
Witness the sugarcoated, diamond-
Decorated, pearl-bedecked estuaries,

The access and ingress of dreams,
The orifice that leads home
To whatever vanishing wisdom
There is for prearranged encounters.
Her mouth strung out in frost
Blew rings of smoke, her lips cracked from the cold,
Made us wonder, why not use a softener?
She whispered smoking was her vice, she loved it,
More than living, and she would
Damn well die before quitting.
We could have loved her,
But the smoke smell, and the rotting
Molar in her dead mouth, the foul odor made hard work
Of kissing, and besides, all of those piercings
Got in the way, perhaps deliberately.
There was a garnish of Viking dew
Around my lips, tongues slurping across my face,
Feminine saliva glory, phrasing
Languid communiqués of split-level
Fabrication. I saw him in the upper left
Corner of the hall, black wings extended,
Casting streetwise shadow, and giddily
Thought to myself, so this is hell.

Amen created the teeth

10. The Teeth

If meaning should be looked for,
Why not in teeth, Amen!
They have left their mark everywhere,
And the earth has no choice
But to remember them ruefully.
All of her landscape modified,
For teeth to rip the fruit and leaf,
Nature's fix for the predator and omnivore,
Chewing forgetfully, carelessly

Dribbling excess onto a butcher's apron.
Nothing in any body survives
Longer than teeth. My pincers shuttle
From end to end of this box, full of what used to be
A human. Bones murmured in brown ooze
Yield solid white enamel, slated for drilling
To extricate the pure gene strands.
Every morning the dreadful work,
Reminding me of my destiny,
An intuitive knowledge that something is wrong,
Subsequent discovery that residues
Of leprosy and tuberculosis are curtained
Within the disintegrating grunge.
Only the great late vitamin M, Misogyny,
Could have invented *Vagina dentata,*
Nightmare of attic assignation,
Micro-atomic bombs in your crotch,
Oh when will I be the object of your caresses?
The wonder of berries and grapes
Bursting under the bite,
Explosion of taste on the palate,
A joyride down into the body,
The crack of chocolate held in your cupped hand,
The guestbook for delicacies, flaked out on the sofa,
Crackle of popcorn, butter and salt—
You could not find love,
Could not hoist your bum from the gorge,
Could not fill the void in your middle,
So here you are, gathering profundity
Into the fullness of your belly.

Ibikan created the molars

11. The Molars

Not being the sharpest canine
On a gum, Ibikan failed to notice

That molars are also teeth.
Questing for cement, pulp, dentine,
Enamel in all of the deep volcanoes,
He emerged from his expedition
Looking like a white pickaninny in blackface,
Then, slapping together what had been retrieved,
Created the pustule upon which
All future root canals were inflicted
And from which all teeth of wisdom
Were ruthlessly extricated.
Perhaps they were not there in the first place,
Like grass and leaves, and these destined
To be chewed at length by the monsters
Who developed in the skulk of time,
Wearing great canines in their faces
And ravaging the evolving apical meristems
Innocently trying their hand at growth,
And these ruminants themselves
Becoming belly substance
For the greatest monster of all.
He inherited the pains well known
To King Harald of old, who hesitated
To follow St. Gregory's ancient prescription,
Not knowing about clove powder
And coconut oil promoted by freaks of the organic.
How do they absorb the right-wing slogans,
Cascading over certain tongues like whitewater boomers
Over a well-churned river futon?
A decently appointed back molar,
Even when cracked and reduced to one half,
Can survive for decades. Poor chalcolithic invalids,
In the care of expert bead crafters
Wielding bow drills, mouths ripped open,
Drilling out the tooth worms, fillings of bees wax.
Now that my tooth is repaired,
What shall I do about the fractured
And dislocated jaw bone?

Basiliademe created the tonsils

12. The Tonsils

First order of defense against the merry pathogens
Perambulating down the weed-smoke path.
An esoteric type, Basiliademe,
Who liked looking down-throat
With his poker mace head.
No defense against zingers
Heading in either direction.
Hold all strep bacteria and viruses,
Their symptoms endless.
You are the tonsil of my eye,
Two blobs thrown on a zinc table
After horrific extraction,
And why of the twelve children
Did only four survive?
Because living out there,
No doctors, no scientific tweezers
Against the virus-catching blobs,
Against the flow of pathogenic writ.
My breath comes in skunk savor
As long as there is a wheeze in my swoop.
My throat the Encyclopedia of Sludge,
The vocals indeterminate as to size,
Concerned with quantitative whinge
As opposed to qualitative serve.
This hinges on the existence
Of civilizations, the mood of the moment
Devastating erudite stratagems,
Twisting the truth to live another day.
The metaphysic of the tonsil!
On the last Day of Judgment
They will be lined against the wall,
Organs of torture imported from their morass to the brick,
Standing before the Angel of the Biotic,

Lacking the organs to wail,
Awaiting the vengeance for crimes
Against the human throat.
And no one will play the piano
When they are annihilated *in omne tempus,*
Never again to swell and choke the anthropoid host.

Achcha created the uvula

13. The Uvula

Not the soft palate, not the hard palate,
No, the Uvula! Let us consider
The juncture when something transpired
That had never transpired before:
The uvula opted for exit.
Readying itself for opportunity,
Someone proclaimed the name Achcha!
And the uvula jetted out,
Landing on milady's décolletage,
Precipitating a moue the likes of which
Have sent a thousand warriors
Upon well-known insanities.
The soft palate,
Communicating with the hard palate
(By way of saliva, super-spy of cavities),
About confinement of the uvula.
Nothing harder for the armature
As when a member studies rebellion
And begins growing hysterically.
The offender is pierced,
Infusing gag reflex of Homeric proportion.
Where with the moist food,
No marker in middle-road,
Pointing the way?
Food passes over, breath, burning liquid,
Hum in the crackling cold.

Let me regale you, uvula,
With strawberries, melted Swiss cheese,
Peanut butter and jelly on French rye.
Vibrato of an opera diva.
The man of the house looking for a horse,
Needing its tail for tying off that thing
In his son's throat.
Expertly shaping the lasso,
One single horse hair, snip!
Disregard future snoring,
When child becomes man,
Keeping awake his wife
And all fornicating in-laws.

Adaban created the neck

14. The Neck

Adaban created the site of hickeys;
Humans have died from less.
In young women, gentle curve of the nape,
Delicately bordered in beautiful geishas,
In older men, rilled scruff spilling
Over starched collars, unmistakable
Emblem of corporate power.
Target also for judo chops.
The Adam's apple stuck
Between vertebra C2 and 3,
Stopping air flow and the need
For any further unemployment benefit.
Impacted from the other side,
Whiplash by insipid texting
During operation of insubordinate sedan,
Cured by soft collar, enormous indemnification influx.
How do they do it when they sing,
Adam's apple bobbing rapidly
As in *vibrato perfecto,* others without quaver.

Or creating false sobs,
Teary eyes, pouting lips, listing head,
Lugubrious sounds, until a beat is missed,
Shunts liquid into lungs for lengthy choking cough.
Advisable to eat in company,
Lest food, usually by way
Of the esophagus, chooses to stray
Down the trachea; you stand
Pointing, saying nothing, struggling,
Until companion performs Heimlich maneuver.
How else administer five blows,
Five abdominal thrusts from behind?
(Fold these instructions carefully
For back pocket just in case.)
Some knew how to imitate the sounds
Of every creature living in their country,
Frogs to crickets to jackals.
Often suddenly performed, startling foreigners,
As if part of the language, as if they wanted to transport
Their idiom down someone's throat.

Chaaman created the vertebrae

15. The Vertebrae

Unlike the spine of the world,
Like the Milky Way,
No pearl in this necklace can be missed, Chaaman,
A feature of its weakness. One link jeopardized
And the whole body collapses.
The upright curve essential to all bipedal creatures,
Plagued with pains and malady,
Cured with balloons and bone grafts,
The way a gardener grafts his cherry trees,
The repository of stress.
Sorry, old boy, we need to push this needle
Up your spinal cord, and if we administer

Anesthetics, how will we know
The needle is in the right place?
Only your screaming can tell us that.
It is, after all, the anchor for those embracing arms,
In the great trunk of this motile organism,
What holds you together,
The structure behind it all,
Many-storied bone skyscraper
Built in dynamic tension
To avoid the earthquakes.
Go ahead, indulge yourself.
My hand will be there to guide you,
And if you don't want to learn
Playing the piano or the trombone,
Or if you regret not playing them,
Or if your genes favor your father
Instead of your mother who is the smarter one,
Or if you have hair growth
On the wrong type of face,
Or if you suddenly realize
You've met a terrorist
By looking in the mirror,
Or if you discover
That you will never be able to stop lying,
Don't you worry about a thing:
I will always have your back.

Dearcho the throat

16. The Throat

How many angels were playing
This musical instrument? Dearcho and at least
Four others, the reason
It turned out vulnerable. A string of piano wire,
Expertly applied, could slice through the passages
Like a knife through Brie.

The aliens came, looked,
And mused upon so improbable an armature,
Which was able to screech, demand, and subjugate
Its lesser fellows, although what set them apart
Remained a mystery.
Stamping out facsimiles,
Bonk! Bonk! While something in the operator's hand
Shifts slightly at every ejection,
High voice, low voice, gruff, gravelly, sweet, and dumb,
Thick, thin, long, short, and commonplace,
Some tasting drab and bland, some hot and zesty,
All throats that ever were in man or beast.
Go, shout your superiority to all,
A mouthwash gargle of prig and smug,
And should you threaten to forget,
Chase generously with greed and self-esteem.
Has your throat been an open sepulcher,
Or has it been a source of desecration?
Are all your sounds zip-locked,
The ideas you express vacuum-packed
In credos of chauvinism?
The forensic scientist found them there,
When they laid you open for inspection
At the foot of the Pearly Gates.
Saint Peter has this habit
Of stroking his throat when perplexed
At the recklessness of those who seek to enter.
Gargamel could not help gagging
Every time he thought about his failure
To make gold from Smurfs.
Drs. Octopus and Horrible both choked to death
While swallowing a mouse. Believe me, I am sympathetic
To any natural-born miscreant
Failing to control his genes.

Tebar the right shoulder

17. The Right Shoulder

Is the right shoulder of Atlas
Still rocking world and sky, Tebar,
After the wry exchange
From his shoulder to Hercules and back again,
And what of Sisyphus impelling his rock,
Or Sampson dislodging his pillars?
Are these the tasks
That shoulders were designed for?
Young men with tattoos lingering,
Fierce tigers glaring across the world,
Captive heroes in thrall
Attempting giant rocks and pillars,
While maidens glide into their prisons,
Wiping perspiration from their brows,
Loosening the cruel bonds
For a night of moonstruck lust.
Perhaps it's time to embrace
The actual weaknesses of the arms and try
Another path to make-believe.
Before we go on to levitate,
Let us become worthy of ourselves.
You need to hold the ceiling at this end,
So that the other end is fixable.
Everything in your family will take place
Under it, the blooming, the cooling,
The fighting, the peeing on precious rugs,
The times you will need your right shoulder
To burst through the doors,
Behind which your old man is abusing his wife,
The times in which your sister
Becomes as luminescent and as lifeless
As an angel extracting your ancient history

From the morass of all harm,
The times your brother floats to the ceiling
That you have been holding in your exasperation,
In a dense cloud of weed-scent, bombing himself
Through all the imaginary swarms
Of stinging bees.

N...the left shoulder

18. The Left Shoulder

In spite of the creator's anonymity,
This is where the violin belongs.
Once more high culture foiled
At the south end, not bearing the globe,
Not shoving through the door like a bull,
But one shoulder searching
For someone's head to support,
For the instrument to rest against,
That brings joy to a stark minority.
The clavicle a bulwark,
A strut from shoulder blade to sternum,
Favorite perch for devils plotting a soul's corruption.
Will this clavicle bear the horizontal shove
Impending always from the heaving
And tugging of the orbiting arena?
Those beads in your left pocket,
How often do you have to worry them?
On the left side of the road
I should always be on your left,
To discourage the wild bike-riders
From snatching your purse.
The rest of me is too off-color
For anyone's jurisdiction.
Walking through the waterfall,
Right shoulder front, left shoulder
Tangential curve diverting

A cascade, the spill of rudeness and ill temper,
And afterwards when digging the graves
Heave soil over the left,
High and beyond the accumulated pyramid.
Anyone using my body from now on
Will have to be in the virtual.
You can use my head to think,
My eyes to see your own outrages,
My ears to hear your sharps and flats,
My mouth to say and taste whatever vinegar remains
From sleeping on your left side,
While looking at the other pillow
And spying there a lady of the lounge
You've never seen before.

Mniarchon the right elbow

19. The Right Elbow

Are we measuring in Ells today,
Or cubits, Mniarchon, where the whole
Complicated contraption is nicely covered
In skin. No membranes, ligaments, muscles
To be seen, no bones fitting exactly
One into the other, and, if not,
Painful dislocation of the humerus,
Radius, and mandatory ulna.
My head was heavier than customary
After colliding with profligate midnight,
Right hand propping up chin,
Right elbow finding a place among
Tangled objects that have lived on tabletop
Since Frou-Frou danced at Maxim's.
The left is cold-cocking a scholarly lady,
Trying to explain the relevancy of apostolic heresy.
Tug in the mind, painful compromise,
The horse veered off the track.

Yet, plowing through crowd in train or theater,
There is work in tandem, shoving aside
Like-minded clientele, propelling
Forward with exaggerated keenness,
Attempting to find a pageant of buffoons,
To take the dazzling footlight off itself;
Manspreading goes with it,
The elbows flaked uncaring where buried,
In whose midriff. How many bus rides,
Sitting with elbows jabbing at your abdomen,
Trying to concoct my phobias anew!!—
I avoid them by taking hold of the fall.
Long ago, anything was a threat
Until I grabbed and turned it into a decorated swing.
Whenever I fell through the floors,
Through the oscillating space,
I wound up gently falling into pink cotton,
Shouting with loud and freaky voice
At the startled demons,
Hey, hey! Don't overreact to the hit men
I'm sending your way!

…e the left elbow

20. The Left Elbow

Dr. …e! Dr. …e! Something is lying next to me
In my bed, claiming to be my left elbow!
I have not seen it before,
Do not want it for a partner in sex,
Am unwilling to share my plow or my fork,
Will not be tethering the object to my foot or waist
Or, if straightened, will not utilize it
To point at a swarm of swallows
Nor allow it to wield a sword in my defense.
Remove the disturbance at once!
It interferes with all my decisions;

I cannot find the right balance for the other side.
Your hand on my, as you say,
Left elbow, even though you have to admit,
Isn't mine, if you wish to touch the object,
Be my happy visitant. I cannot claim it
Myself; it has never accomplished anything
At my behest, and if it asserts itself
To the contrary, I disavow all attainment.
There will be no receipt of awards
Or medals, the ugly thing is more lined
Than anything that can be construed
As me; funny how I have an affinity
For the hand at the end of it, but not for mid-angle—that
Would be going too far.
The funeral for "that" elbow will be tomorrow,
Only a few friends who have promised
To attend. Am I being extreme?
But it isn't mine, and it's beginning
To atrophy. *Rigor mortis*
Is just around the corner.
You would never transport
All of your deceased relatives around,
Wherever you went, would you?
It had no will to live longer,
Had stopped bending to and fro,
And simply lay, an alien,
Cast off and down my left side.

Abitrion the right underarm

21. The Right Underarm

It was all done with the appropriate
Decorum, through all the four stages
Of axillary hair, but stealing some
Of the testosterone used to form the testicles.
Abitrion troweled the curve

With one graceful sweep,
Knowing that underarm hair dyeing
Would at some stage be the rage
And inconceivable riches would be amassed
To keep the tiniest body whiff concealed.
The artist must attain his canon,
No nonpareil, but the gentle
Vagueness of a Cezanne daub.
It was a condition of higher request
That the range was so restricted.
The underarm only? Should it not have been
A part of the right arm, or the right shoulder?
Were forces underway,
Trying to sabotage this very Adam,
This supposed paragon of all human bodies following?
The "expert" angels were too layered, standing three deep
Around the agonized creature,
And Tebar, in the grips of boredom,
Who was supposedly creating the right shoulder,
Began to carve decorations into the bone.
For a time, the body could not find
Its borders, began drifting
In and out, where nothing remained
Except a fragment of right underarm,
A formless patch of skin
With flesh attached, and tufts of hair.
The makers cried out,
Pulling back their singed fingers,
Shaking them away from the field of thought-creation.
Should they have been standing in saltwater,
Or on the rocks of a hot volcano?
Until this day, no historian has found
A valid explanation for mold or setting.

22. The Left Underarm

Botox is needed, Euanthen! I haven't tried this area yet!
And why are there towels lying and drying all over
Your messy apartment—
Or should I have used acupuncture
Instead? Is it because of the sweat,
Sweetie? You're so self-conscious
About the silliest things. Take off your shirt;
If you're not careful, it will start dripping on the carpet.
Or perhaps acupressure?
The fabric has given you a rash.
Maybe a chiropractor.
Is that why you were so obsessive
About creating, of all things, a left underarm?
If there isn't a spat, there will be a spot
In which the least important will be the preeminent,
And what is hidden shall be exposed.
Did you deliberately add those hidden glands
For scent production, so that all of these populations
Would come into existence?
Women swooning helplessly
At the hint of a whiff?
What could be more decisive at 3 a.m.
Than pheromonology?
Why try to spook composure?
Perhaps if I hang some garlic
In the kitchen door?
Because I refuse control or dominance
By something so subliminal.
Does knowledge offset leverage?
When I first caught your body fragrance,
I knew! You can't blame me
If one day, when you come close,
Leaning in and placing your ear

On my belly, listening to my breath,
Feeling its homey cadence,
Suddenly you will hear something else,
Like a tiny knock from the inside.

Krus the right hand

23. The Right Hand

Thank you, Krus, for this minimum,
For not turning me into a crab
With cantilevered claw, the integrated concept
Of opposable thumbs, the ability to demonstrate
X, Y, and Z-axes, thumbs up,
Thumbs down, victory sign,
And uncounted other semaphores.
My right hand has spoken to me in the night,
Because it is the culmination
Of vectors, crossing from the left
Brain hemisphere through the chest
And down the right arm. It babbles
Nervously after major effort,
Such as wielding a hammer for the rock,
Or lifting a hundredweight of fishmeal
Up to the right shoulder.
Is it possible I could be mix-handed?
My right gravitates naturally to a pen,
My left instinctively to a baseball or pebble
To cast over water. If right-handers
Are supposed to be gifted in all-around
Cognitive skills, and left-handers in music and math,
Where do I fit? Have I just now
Discovered my brain's predicament?
Slow in everything, gifted in oblivion,
Neither in here nor out there,
Hemming and hawing in the high seas of mediocrity,
Because my right hand can't throw a ball.

Because Adam's right hand
Reached out and took what was offered
By a feminine left, according
To the ancient misogynists.
How many right hands does it take
To make a lunatic out of a well-born child,
Especially when that hand is holding
A cane? Therein lies the origin
Of all trouble, one trauma,
And the world is changed,
One lousy apple bitten,
And a million-church perversion.

Beluai the left hand

24. The Left Hand

As soon as it was fashioned
By Beluai, the left hand decided
To be a slob. Favored by the erudite,
It played in stratospheres
And turned them into distracted geeks,
Allowing initial payoff equal
To that of crocks and tame
Elevator attendants. Ideational trouble,
Elsewhere and distant, was suddenly
Pulled close to the vest, behind a stuttering,
Dyslexic brain, right hemisphere.
Without thinking, some acts
Are right-hand acts, even if they are
Accomplished by the left hand,
The hand that quasi-precociously
Triggered the bitter-almond smell
Of Zyklon B at Auschwitz, thinking
Sanctimoniously it was doing the world
A favor. The hand that unleashed
The first atomic bomb, that kept

Assassinating the best and mollycoddling
The worst, setting the fires at witch burnings,
Crashing airliners into skyscrapers.
There is no better left hand than one that plays
Beethoven sonatas or Brahms intermezzos,
That wields a wild and courageous paintbrush,
Conducts a seven member orchestra as though
Conducting great phenomena in the universe.
Restoring ancient stone walls, he takes a rock in his left,
Hammers it with the right, uses the smaller pieces
To prop and stop up larger stones.
Sometimes the stone refuses,
Bites into the left palm with razor-sharp edges
Now deeply scarred.
No one has ever convinced him
To wear gloves.

Treneu the fingers of the right hand

25. The Fingers of the Right Hand

Those icy fingers up and down my spine
Appear to have lost their iciness,
Welcome to the Pyrocene, Treneu!
You had to send them puttering,
Building machines that went puff-puff,
And now we have entered upon a period
Of refutation and derangement,
But don't get too used to the earth
As it is, because it won't be.
The desert was always close, and now you'll win it,
Sand, storms, hurricanes, and any other
Turbulence! Acceleration of improbability.
How does 300 degrees Fahrenheit grab you?
There we were, sitting separately
In our deep vault, like frozen effigies,
While up at the top the brittle population

Went puff-puff, snuffed out
Like candles by a wet finger.
Spontaneous combustion. Instantaneous
Obliteration. Precooked fingertips.
Goggle-eyed skeletons.
Every sixteen-year-old needs a car!
Every blacktop needs a race!
Every highway intersection needs a jam!
The air, the air is everywhere!
All that flooding, and all those tornadoes
And hurricanes at once; while half the house
Went flying off, I was thinking
Nobody would believe this if you told them,
Because what's happening is just too improbable.
I was thinking (as my library upstairs and downstairs
Went flying off to the west) maybe I ought to change
The way I think about what can happen,
Maybe the probable or possible have been
Expanded, along with the impossible,
And if the impossible merges
With the possible, how shall I ever
Acclimatize myself to my present
Sitz im Leben?

Balbel the fingers of the left hand

26. The Fingers of the Left Hand

My apologies to the left thumb
(Ostensibly made by Balbel)
For using it to gouge out a defenseless eye.
My apologies to the index finger
For all of its accusatory activities;
To the middle finger
For communicating profane defiance;
To the ring finger for symbolizing all of the ill-advised
Dalliances that have brought us to where we are;

To the pinky for its name and uselessness,
Except for insertion into a nostril.
How are the left-hand goats
Separated from the right-hand sheep?
What is their reaction
When lightning strikes the cathedral?
Does the left hand really want to be
The left hand all of the time,
Or only at four in the morning?
I apologize to the left hand
For placing it into the traps that fall forward.
Or into cauldrons of acid,
Coming up chewed and fleshless.
Or allowing it to vanish
Into woodchoppers and electrical outlets.
Or promoting sustained use in relentless factories,
Where saw-toothed machines
Stamp out their facsimiles,
Often taking a few fingers along for the ride,
So that you have crowds of retired Republicans
Running around with mangled hands,
Half their fingers missing.
A person so damaged
Attains to a form of invincibility.
Once hurt, twice hurt,
There is little that anyone can do to them.
Mangled left hands (or right hands),
Have too long been threats
To America's democracy and lifestyle.

Krima the fingernails

27. The Fingernails

Krima of the refined claw.
There is a sense of desperation,
Thinking about the nails.

Sense of panic in childhood,
When the teacher asked
For extended hands.
After pitching bales of hay,
Mowing grain with a sickle,
Hoeing infinite beet rows,
And shoveling, frankly, cow shit,
Where did they get off
Asking for immaculate fingernails?
The water unsanitary,
That gave you worms and who knows what,
The food just barely sufficient
For a good dose of malnutrition,
And this is what worried them,
Certainly not the white spots
Lodged in the keratin like the polka dots
On a Kusama sculpture.
Right of center,
Or perhaps in the middle of the middle
Of the bull's eye,
A virtual pinky fingernail, surviving solely
On a drug named stricture,
Or possibly realpolitik,
Which was not in the eye of the bull.
Gnawing teeth have broken in
Whatever you want this fingernail to be.
Flying at a Persian rug,
Half-moon-shaped fingernail, clipped off.
They have found their rightful place
Between the flosser and the utility knife.
My shoulder blades are still humming
From nails dug in, well-documented evidence
That something glorious happened
Last night.

Astrops the right breast

28. The Right Breast

I would not, Astrops,
Begin with the right breast of Adam;
I would go straight to Eve.
You have sinned greatly in that regard, never
Finding the perfect shape,
But meandering between the undersized
To the exaggerated,
From the roving east/west, ranging side set,
Grieving tear-dropped, gliding
Slender, flowing bell-shaped,
Negotiating asymmetric, to the idyllic round.
What is so secret about Victoria?
Keep your eyes on the eyes
And listen to her words.
How did we get from Roman breastbands
(Not to enhance but to flatten)
To the Medieval chemise without pants,
Shirts with bags for the breasts?
Nothing but economics.
Women were too poor to own a pair of drawers,
And if they wore them they were considered bold.
Celebration of baby lips as the ultimate niche
For purest libido,
A composition poorly understood.
The ass of a man
In all men propounded,
Their chests now wasted,
Each one a collapse on the way,
And the beginning of feminine design
Under chest hair.
The breasts of Aphrodite,
The shores of Mykonos,
Heave under his chin.
Two bubbles wearing warts,

And streaking around them
His drunken breath.
Don't show yourselves to anyone,
He yells inaudibly,
My testosterone is leaking out!

Barroph the left breast

29. The Left Breast

Barroph's mother informed him
That his creation would not initiate
The end of days, but it might as well have.
She told him that it would never be sweeter,
Even if he poured in all the sugar in the world,
Because there would be nowhere to flee
When all the fault-finding jeremiads
Came gushing down on him.
That he would be blamed
For the warring civilizations,
For the Babel confusion,
For the creation of the most vulnerable,
Most powerful feminine assets.
She told him they would be
Like two fawns in a meadow,
Or like two clusters in a palm tree,
The tender and forceful.
That queens and nurses would bow down to him
On his return from the Egyptian exile,
And that he would be carried in his nurse's arms,
When, presumably, she would be topless.
That in the sight of these towers,
Clusters, fawns, the seven pillars
Of wisdom would pitch forward.
She told him that pointing
These clusters at the chevron tattoos
Of fleeing abstemious heralds,

A majority of nations would cease all acts of mercy.
That the slowest movement of fawns
Through the chambers of government
Was like watching two mountains
Erode to a flat table.
That if these twin canaries
Came under the microscope,
They would vanish under the eye.
They would shape-shift from particle
To wave, following the well-known principle
Of uncertainty, no matter who was fondling them.

Baoum the right shoulder joint

30. The Right Shoulder Joint

Baoum, the great professor Baoum,
Inventor of ball and socket,
You will have taken the right humerus
In your left, the scapula in the right
And, like Galileo, you will have patiently
Fitted one into the other.
The main problem will have been
The ligaments, and where to place them.
What will have been needed,
Will have been the most mobile joint
In this as yet transfixed anatomy.
Abitrion, who will have been distracted
Momentarily by Treneu's white rabbit
Sniffing at the underarm that he will have been
Quietly trying to weave into place,
Will clandestinely have allowed his left fingers
To explore the complexities of the astounding
Joint, which will have been engineered
Into abilities that will have included
The swinging of a sword,
The imitation of windmills,

Mountain climbing, pushing a large boulder
Repeatedly up a steep height,
Flying with bee-wax wings.
The ears of the white rabbit
Will have folded all the way back
At Abitrion's touch.
Baoum will have been in corroboration
With the deadliest, most efficient
Spiders in the world, to weave ligament stronger
Than cotton, stronger than linen;
Baoum's entire attitude toward the world will have been
Dorky and lackluster, owing to his designer genius.
He will not have had Abitrion's love of white rabbits,
But an automatic reflex of kicking them into the gutter.
He will also have had the very annoying habit
Of thinking in the future perfect tense.

Ararim the left shoulder joint

31. The Left Shoulder Joint

Before Christmas existed, Baoum visited Ararim,
Bringing a gift package: The left shoulder joint of Adam,
Telling him it was a puzzle,
Or so it was claimed in later depositions.
Professor Baoum told his student
Ararim he had one hour
To solve the puzzle. Various parts
Of the left shoulder joint were strewn
All across the pantry. With knitted
Brows sat Ararim, fitting this and that
And wondering how he might
Pass the test. (The professor had already
Discretely distanced himself, knowing
That his student was basically a knucklehead.)
Returning an hour later, Baoum saw
That nothing had been accomplished

And asked his student what he should
Have done. Ararim deduced
That he should have found
The right fit, whereupon he received
A box on the ears. It was
Astringently put to him that
Thinking comes before fitting.
Professor Baoum then disclosed
All of his ball-and-socket secrets,
And even lent his deadly spider
To weave the tendons.
Nevertheless, the mechanism
Had been assembled by an amateur
And was for all time the statistically lesser joint.
When Ararim himself became a venerable personage,
He was haunted by these early ventures,
It was as though his life had been penciled
In lead, like the Russian scientists,
Who always worked in pencil,
And in the high schools, in which the author
Was strictly divided from his work,
Where pencil had become de rigueur.
All your errors would then be forever
Fixed in lead.

Areche the belly

32. The Belly

Areche, for the world of the internal.
To negotiate this region of swamp,
To actually see it employed, assimilating
And breaking down what nourishes all else,
There is need to discard carnality
And go swerving into deep bodily niches

By way of headier quintessence.
It is, after all, the center of synergy
And compromise, between macro-
And microorganism. When nature
Is abused, she cries out; indulge in too much
Of a good fare, and you get the runs.
Conversely, it appears that some of the original
Bacteria have confused co-existence
With antipathy, devouring the ecosystem
In which they found their inauguration.
After the introduction of catheters,
Relentlessly shoved down the throat
By several sanitized hands, red blood cells
Drained from the bleeding ulcer
Into the translucent bag, where they
Appeared to turn color. "Coffee,"
The doctors called it. Lucky you weren't a cow,
There would be seven of them,
Or a whale, having to deal
With Jonases. How do you quarter a human body,
When all you're interested in is krill or shrimp?
This is where cringing occurs in earnest,
Where intuition turns tiger and gobbles your brain,
Where anxiety pleats you into an accordion
And plays you like a wailing specter,
Where attraction for someone makes you feast and fast,
As though you were trying to deal with indigestion
And absorption at the same time, and none of these are
Worth it, someone once told me, better to displace them
With emphasis on sinful food,
And never, on threat of eternity's rage,
Never, to use the phrase,
"Belly to belly!"

33. The Navel

If it hadn't been the navel,
Perhaps it might have been something
That creates itself at the point of birth,
Perhaps as a result of cutting
The umbilical cord, so where exactly
Does Phthaue come in?
Was he the creator of a scar,
Left by another process entirely?
According to the most recent research,
The umbilical cord, sporting two arteries
And one vein, conducts food
To the fetus and removes its waste
While in the womb, during which processes
The belly button is nonexistent,
Since it is an integral part of the passage,
And once the fetus is born,
Becomes what it becomes,
A scar, so what exactly was your purpose,
Phthaue? Since Adam was created PDQ,
It stands to reason that he never needed
A navel, and you must have been
The loser in the crowd, standing
Behind those who actually DID something,
While you were jumping around,
Moving your hands, pantomiming effectiveness.
To all the back-to-the-Wombers of the world,
Your postman just deposited an urgent message:
You have a navel! The umbilical cord
Has been cut! You are not protected
Any more by mom, neither your house
Nor your country can be characterized
As a womb! They are a sponge,
Absorbing what is exterior, and to them you are

A passing phantom.
Some dip their toes into the wave,
Some plunge in,
Some stand behind gesticulating,
Dancing in sand and pantomiming
Effectiveness that has never been.

Senaphim the abdomen

34. The Abdomen

Shoving Phthaue aside, the bully
Senaphim proceeded to append
With shamanistic spatula
Whatever surrounded the "navel,"
Piling one muscle on top of the next,
Rendering Adam's midriff ripped.
In later times the Gothic artists painted
Muscles that did not exist,
Till Michelangelo had to practice
Dissection on cadavers to discover
Clandestinely how these brawny
Strata had been assembled.
How powerful, for all time
Demonstrated by the rope-a-dope
Ruse for a Thrilla in Manila.
The ripped and the rocket scientist,
Increase in the one, decrease in the other.
Ripping off his shirt he sat
At the bongos, ripping off
His chains he crashed through
The door and into the cotton field,
He allowed the water to cascade
Over his chest, he gripped the oar
And laid into it, he jumped up
And hit the ball with premeditated

Force, he pressed the weight
At 425, throwing it to the floor
Contemptuously, his attitude
Intimidating those who followed,
And in spite of that there was
A shyness, a lack of confidence
In matters of courtship or affection,
And her taught body, when it curled
Into a sofa, could still feel him
Coursing through her veins,
And wanted to jump up,
Run out into the wild afternoon,
Prove once and for all
That every truth was false,
No matter how true it had been,
Or how old.

Arachethopi the right ribs

35. The Right Ribs

"Now listen," said Arachethopi,
"This is not going to be easy,
Because I'm doing the right ribs,
Zabedo the left, Taphreo the backbone,
And it all has to fit together and around
The spinal cord, which has connections
Going off in every direction.
Watch out for the spinal cord, it sends
Electricity from top to bottom for all
The movements, the other way
For sense of touch throughout the body,
And for automatic reflex, which overrides
Everything. Wear your rubber gloves
Or you won't just short-circuit the entire system
But get a shock that will send you zooming
Across infinity!"

While Taphreo was quickly churning out
T1 through T12, tossing them into the middle,
Zabedo promptly attached the seven true ribs,
But before he could finish, Arachethopi
Had attached the three false and two floating
Ribs, and each homotechnician jumped
Out of the other's way to complete the order;
Those bones had memory,
Especially the rural ones,
Before they got to creak and crack
With arthritis. Back when they
Piled up the fieldstones, hitched up
The bovines and pressed down hard
On the simple plow, straight lines
Between the boundary markers.
Next to the stone clearance pile
There was a pillar stone, witness
To an agreement with the neighbor
Who had sold away a stretch of land
Again marked by long
Boundary walls, the entire landscape
Looking like an extended rib cage,
Some with drainage so poorly
Constructed, the whole country
Was flowing off into the ocean.

Zabedo the left ribs

36. The Left Ribs

While walking through the radiant fall,
A siren voice sounded his name: "Zabedo!"
He stood in shock, being a minor
Angel among towering peers, not
Au courant with voices coming at him
Out of the blue. He hid under a chestnut,
Stumbling slightly over the fallen fruit,

Thinking that he might escape whatever
Accusations had been leveled. "Zabedo!
You have been chosen to fashion the bone
Of Adam's left ribcage!" He tried hard
Not to breathe, hoping it would go away.
But the siren voice insisted, and an invisible
Hand took him by the scruff of the neck
And spirited him to the site of creation.
He tried to stand aside, wondering
Whether he might vanish into the ground,
But Arachethopi, a true loudmouth,
Said, "Now listen!" Proceeding to hold forth
About the correct procedure and how
It was to be accomplished by all the relevant
Participants. Perhaps a gust of smoke,
He thought, but the others began yelling
At him, commanding him to fill the gap
Between right ribs and backbone.
He was persuaded to participate,
Albeit reluctantly, because it was an armor
For the heart that he was building,
With an infusion of smoke, biting both ways,
Enveloping the totality with impenetrable
Mediocrity, that only the very gifted
Would be able to pierce, relegating
The rest into a stupor of the barest
Consciousness, lest they gobble each other up
At the first opportunity, lest they
Overflow with insane ideas and conflicts,
Lest they scream constantly about themselves
In perpetual self-promotion, lest they
Drown in such vehemence or apathy
As to blindly wander off a cliff.

37. The Right Hip

It was certainly an exceptional
Undertaking to embark upon. Something
Not only to catch your breath,
But to change it. To create a silence
Within, although there were no tools.
While hands are perfectly acceptable
As appliances, they task the mental
Powers. Why not have a rasp, at least,
Or a tiny saw, perhaps a small chisel
And a screwdriver? They did not say,
Barias, we shall now construct
A hologram, or a flat screen. This
Was real, and honest work was required,
Because it would have to go its own way
For all the following centuries. Because
Once it walks out of this décor,
It will forget us, block us out, as though
It had undergone an unforgivable
Trauma, and there is only so much you can do with bone.
If you ever figured out the dynamic tension
Of a simple leg movement, it would blow you
Out of your kneeling pew.
Segue to the following:
Sitting in one of the better hotels
Of Cairo, the American delegation
Looked up at the zigzagging stairway
And saw a surprisingly modern
Wedding procession, making its way
Toward them one step at a time.
In front of the bride and groom
An extremely healthy looking
Young lady, who belly-danced

In bare attire, ascending and descending a few steps
At a time, and periodically accosting
The groom by whispering into his ear,
Always making him guffaw, and following each sortie
With a brazen shake of her right hip.
Profane advice, whispered into the ear of the groom,
With a huge dose of smuttiness,
A custom as old as the pharaohs.

Phnouth the left hip

38. The Left Hip

Holy Christopher and all his ankle biters, me,
Phnouth, the unfortunate one, I hoisted a few
Last night, Holy Mother Joe and all the gigolos of Tennessee,
Of course I didn't hoist anything *you* might imagine,
But admittedly, I couldn't put a screw into the nut,
And now they want me to fit this hip thing into the scrapula,
I mean the hurerus or turerus, some disease that usually
Follows the schooners of New Guinea in the form of nuts and bolts,
Which do not have to be fitted at all, or screwed in for that matter,
Although it does involve screwing. I must be mad signing up for this.
Where is my hifflomotapus?! Did I say what I didn't hoist any of?
Nothing that hasn't been invented yet. You there, off the starboard
Scrapula, Baraiyas, was it? Where is your turerus? Are you finished
Screwing it yet? Joe Christopher and my holy mother,
Stop running away with the body!
Doesn't every room need a hifflomotapus? You are
A devious little cherub, so don't you dare anphrotomorthize me,
The last time I could still see my pinkie, I was an angel,
Even though I did hoist a few, and I don't know what happened
To my halo. Don't say word one. What happened to my pulse?
Does he have a pulse yet? All in chunks and pebbles.
How many parts of him are there? A hundred? A thousand? A billion?
Hi there hippy thing, meet the turerus, your very own turerus.
Hey, turerus, if you don't leave immediately,

You will wear out your welcome. No mom-and-pop
Hotels for you here! And don't steal any
Mountains on your way out! Wait, wait!
Catch that turerus, don't let it get away!
Not enough hippy turerusses makes them
Conclude how many welcomes do you
Want me to be? May all your sea life
Thrive like hammered catfish. Why are we not talking
As if we were angels? When did I become a hifflomotapus?
Let go my arm! I turerus you in the name of New Guinea
And Joe Christopher—stop the bus!
Stop churning the butter! My scrapula
Is pirouetting around your chunks and pebbles,
Your pinkie round and round.
Every room needs a hifflomotapus pinkie!

Abenlenarchei the marrow

39. The Marrow

Red cells, white cells, I need
To flow, this difficult secular medium,
Asleep, without consciousness,
No gilded thrones, not positioned
In the name of anyone, not even
Like glass, the glass idea nonviable,
Ejected, held captive by the hardened
Carapace, unseen and overlooked,
Like the cupule of the oak, the carapace a silo,
To the body like milk and sugar.
Up in the rustling crown, a call,
Abenlenarchei! The marrow for
This body! And down I flowed
Into the very core, at lightning speed,
Stopped short at the left hip,
Where did it go? Why was it

Not in place? The pelvic bone,
The femur, absent from the frame,
Then suddenly snapped into place,
Did they not know, my medium
Formless, no consciousness,
Needing the premeditated vessel to hold it,
Like a canoe in calm waters,
Who lambasted the sap in this body?
Did they want to mix in errors?
But it is I who will be lying in the grave
Within this skeleton, my essence
Passed on to the offspring;
Always I shall be caught in the talons
Of an eagle, as everything is caught
In someone's claws, and this essence
Is neither good nor evil, it wants
To build and heal, it wants to be
Useful and pass away in its own
Time. I am like the tears you lose
When laughing, when crying,
Nowhere at home, at constant need to flow,
And may the Almighty save us
From obstructions and from
Unjustified dismemberment.

Chnoumeninorin the bones

40. The Bones

Outrageous! It was outrageous!
Barias motioned to me, placing his finger
Over his lips for silence. The profligate
Phnouth crashed into the site
Of our creation like a mad lowlife
Janitor looking for dust. We knew

At once that he had been waylaid
By sirens, too weak to resist
Their ruinous charms. He flailed
About his allocation, supposedly
The assemblage of the left hip,
Yelling blasphemies and sending
The femur careening across
The empyrean vault and into
The upper heavens. Barias motioned
To me holding the frame in place,
While I rushed after the errant
Constituent, gliding upward
In pursuit of the powerfully flung
Bone like a curly-coated retriever,
Dashing through the lower two
Heavens until I was surrounded
By pearls and dazzling stones,
Accosted by the servants and voices
Of Joseph and Azrael. I threw
My net and caught what I was after,
Not looking left or right,
Dove back down through the dizzying
Murk of stratospheres, straight
For the site, snapping the lost article
Into place as soon as I had arrived,
Relieving Barias of his liability.
Meanwhile we held the degenerate,
forcing him beneath the earthly realm, where
The spirits received him like a lord of hosts.
Indisposed and unqualified for the task,
We wondered what power had certified him for it.
We could but muse upon such folly,
Which introduced intentional impurities
Into a work of creation that ought
To have been perfect.

Gesole the stomach

41. The Stomach

This will require a very tight DNA
Weave, said Gesole to his assistants.
The most resilient area in the body,
It will have to withstand
The acid that breaks down
Everything that comes to the bottom
Of the esophagus. It must be held
In its place when there is panic,
Although in extreme situations
Vomiting is allowed. Let us not formulate
Vacuous propositions about the seven-fold
Exemplar of the cow. We have
An omnivore to assemble, a top
Predator, he will need his intuition
To survive. Before the brain is aware,
The stomach must know what will happen,
And in certain conditions it must
Stop the mouth from articulating.
You all know Meniggesstroeth,
Who was assigned by powers unknown
To produce a brain. Why this
Unmentionable simpleton at such
A complex charge, we cannot know.
We can only try to fill the lacunae
That others have deliberately inserted
Into the labyrinth. Smoothly now,
The exterior a pear-shaped feature
Linking to the small intestine.
They will abuse it incessantly,
Drink of dreadful spirits, stuff
Themselves with garbage,
Screech like ogresses when the body
Rebels, continue abusing even as they

Disintegrate. We cannot be
Responsible for such carrion feeders.
We can build the hull, plank
By plank, and send her off,
Into the waves of the infinite,
And there she's on her own.
Self-inflicted torpedoes
Are not our business.

Agromauma the heart

42. The Heart

Now listen, said Agromauma
To his assistants, no matter what
You may have heard, this is
The most important organ
In the body! It will pump blood
One hundred thousand times
A day, and two billion times
In a life. It can never stop,
Because stopping is death!
We have an absolutely exquisite
Plan of the motor, two sided,
With four valves. One valve opens,
The other one closes, and there is
No backflow, the blood is pushed
Around the body with unbelievable
Force, we remove garbage, we supply
Oxygen and food everywhere. The heart
Is a lion, bodily companion to the soul,
All other organs bound and tethered
To it, dependent, comatose, perceiving
Themselves nurtured only as in a dream.
Now watch the warriors who disdain
Weapons, as they feel carefully, searching

For the precise spot to target,
That will kill an opponent. Design
The most exquisite mechanism
In the universe, and instantly
Alternative creatures will crawl from
Their burrows to destroy the sum
Total of creation. If we have devised
A pure heart, how many circumstances will arise
To poison and contaminate our work?
This is the work of death. Whatever
You give will become a theft, the eyes
Will steal from the brain, the brain
Will steal from the heart, the heart's
Lover will be too confused to remember
Whether his pants are unzipped,
Or what he's been trying to say
While imitating a drowning socialite.

Bano the lungs

43. The Lungs

A wrongful bequest, this!
For as long as I have existed,
I had my heart set on the heart.
Now it has been given to one
Without passion, a drudge
Automaton, who will do his work
With unimaginative competence.
I hear him boasting about the importance,
The centrality of the device that his
Crew is assembling. Perhaps I would
Have taken the same approach, although
On the face of it, the lungs are no less
Important. Does he imagine a human
Can live without breath? What for instance
Is the favorite manner of suicide?

Is it not hanging, the cessation of breath?
Stopping a heart would not even
Come to mind. Oxygen in, carbon dioxide
Out, primary, secondary, tertiary bronchi,
Bronchioles, alveoli, cardiac notches,
How is this organ less complex
Than the heart, and less susceptible
To abuse? A day will come when
Lungs are ripped out of one cadaver
To be installed into another,
Having abused the temple of the body
To such extremes as to willfully
Assemble the coffin. Bovine tears
Will gush like mountain creeks
When the self-abuser discovers that
His physicians have contrived
To add a few more years
To his pitiful life. We are his true
Mirror, wasting long supernatural
Intervals on futile tasks.
Whoever thought that I, Bano,
Would be flopped into this celestial
Sandbox, adding molecule after
Molecule to this aesthetically
Nondescript pair of sponges?

Sostrapal the liver

44. The Liver

Jammed it in there, kaplunk!
Gotta do things with confidence,
And style, see? I'm the lowlife
Around here, the lowlife angel.
If they come and ask me to do this
Or that, I do it just so. I do it
Like a guy on a mission,

He comes into the hotel lobby
And there's a whole bunch of people
Standing around a guy on the floor.
He pushes them aside and shoves
A pencil into the guy's throat,
You know, to make a hole so the air
Can flow. This is not something
A normal person would be able
To do. They would rather stand back
And watch. See, an intellectual type operator
Would be intimidated by all this
Small and hidden stuff, because
It's, like, under cover, where nobody really
Knows what you're doing,
Nobody's even aware that something
Is happening, but *everything*
Is happening! And that is not
How intellectual types operate.
When they do something,
Everybody has to go ooh and aah,
And it has to be described in detail
On the front page of the *Times*,
And they have to be awarded
With the Nobel Prize. That is not
How lowlife thugs operate. They
Do their work where nobody
Can see it, like, under cover.
So, you wanna know something
About the liver? I tell you what,
My local university has some
Excellent courses in Pre-med.
From me you'll be lucky to get
Egy nagy nulla vagy.

Anesimalar the spleen

45. The Spleen

The spleen rebelled, saying,
"I do not do well in unjustified
Confinement. Get someone else
To handle your iron and be your
Blood bank and healer, and let me
Loose!" I stood rooted in shock;
Nothing like this had ever happened before.
Indignation welled up in me. "Where
Would you like to be established,"
I yelled, "On the forehead,
On the chin, or maybe on the ears?
A vile cancerous growth
To beautify our virginal Adonis?"
I gave it two quick slaps,
"I have a huge cleaver
In my back pocket," I said.
"And I can chop you up
Into little pieces. You'll make
Wonderful shark food!
This is the only existence
You'll ever have, lackey!
Get used to it!" This, after I had
Respectfully stepped aside to allow
The gangster Sostrapal to jam his
Liver into the abdomen, in case
His act might hurt the precious
Spleen! I swept it up in my hand,
Threatening to do the same,
And felt it cringing in fear.
Just before impact I stopped
And carefully placed the organ,
Without any more guff.

Reason enough for any craftsman
To hesitate rendering participation.
But there was a work offering
Larger than any self.
Now I feel as though I had planted
A mole onto the perfect diamond.
Reversing the metaphor,
It is like placing a diamond ring
Onto a leprous, withered hand.

Thopithro the intestines

46. The Intestines

So, you needed plumbing,
And you called on Thopithro.
How to harness for maximum
Benefit every type of food
Ever envisioned? When I had
Laid it out, all the companions
Shook their heads, convinced
That Thopithro had gone mad.
Twenty-five feet of piping,
To be installed into a slender
Body. How? We affixed the pipe
Seamlessly to the side of the stomach,
Then slowly in zigzag weave,
We installed the small intestine,
Filling a major cavity in the lower
Torso, and had almost reached the end,
When suddenly the totally drunken
Phnouth crashed into the site!
I tried to ignore everything
That happened around me, focusing
On the complex work at hand,
But my hand slipped during the crash.

Nevertheless, the large intestine,
Sweeping up in ascent, then transverse,
Then descent, majestically framed
The system. Only a small ragged end
Protruded at the joint, where some
Of the material had ripped. This was
A useless appendage, an imperfection,
Which was later termed "Appendicitis."
We could not proceed anew, could hardly
Pull the whole thing out again.
How many deaths did this small detail
Cause in the species we had created?
Don't blame me! You know the culprit!
He should have been assigned
To the fallen, which indeed he was.
But the cosmos has a wish to taste
The bodies that we made,
As though they were chocolate fudge.

Biblo the kidneys

47. The Kidneys

I had my lackeys
To do the work,
While I hovered and floated,
Watching every detail.
They set their hearts on pairs,
As though we were witnesses
For a marriage. Very well,
We manufactured two.
Even the kidney shape,
When oval would have done,
After all, a mere station
In the plumbing system,
Clarification of liquid, blood

And urine, bla bla bla.
And when do you think
Splendor will descend
Upon this humble opus?
I really must get on
With the camouflaging
Of dark matter, to keep
Future scientists occupied
In meaningful careers.
I've seen the vision
Of our clairvoyants,
It haunts the members
Of this heavenly crew.
It is bleak and hideous.
All that we have assembled
Will be compromised.
These kidneys are targeted
For lack of liquid,
Or surfeit of wrong liquid,
The one causing stones,
The other incremental breakdown.
Is this a prognosis
For happiness in marriage?
How rewarding could it be
To tie flowers onto a rhinoceros?

Roeror the sinews

48. The Sinews

We were proletarians,
The crew with the sinews,
And they never thought
Of giving us an hourly wage.
Blue collars all around, and I the shop steward.
One of these days we're gonna strike

For a better salary! Naa, just kidding.
We learned that spider trick from Baoum,
The guy with the shoulders,
Who thinks he owns invention,
Even if the spiders did the job.

Now, that thing that happened
At the Jabbok? Jacob wrestling
With one of the low-lifes?
When he got his hip sinew
Screwed up? I want this to be
Perfectly clear, none of our crew
Had anything to do with that.
We don't do no sabotage;
We take pride in our elbow grease.
'Cause it ain't just sinew to muscle,
It's bone-to-bone, things you need
To move, to dance a jig, to run
A race, or lift a bag of grain.
We'd been weaving it for such as deer,
And elk, and bear, ever since they came
On the old whereabouts and wherever.
Our latest Joe Blows used all of them
For making weapons, like bows.
What a thing, using your own
Body strings to make heat, and using
That heat to hunt more of you, for
More body strings and more meat.
Hey, I didn't say nothin'.
But sometimes you just wonder
Whether all of this wasn't planned,
Somehow? You know, by the big
Honcho? And how can you ever know
That what you're doing is for the best?

49. The Backbone

Before there was an S,
There was a backbone.
We took inspiration from the snake,
The sacrum being the triangular head.
We took inspiration from long
Grocery lists, from rituals
Of the numinous,
From amethysts and diamonds,
Galactic structures, universal chaos,
Unexplained tears and tantrums,
From chaste love, and profane love,
Contrasts in moon and sunshine,
The sweat of the worker,
The indolence of the bureaucrat,
The contrast in God the stone,
God the figurine, and God the beggar,
From voices woven into robes,
From stones built into halls,
From rough rock washed into smooth.
We wandered, we were motivated
By migrating nations, by refugees,
By millions of dying children
Innocent of history or knowledge,
By their plunging echo,
By blooming almond trees,
By the broken word and the broken
Man who uttered it,
By the relentless passing of days,
By all that can be held
Within a human mind,
We took it and lodged it
Deeply in the spine,
The enormous leaky reservoir
Of the unconscious, ruled

By the uncertainty principle,
So that nothing, nothing
Can ever be foretold, including
The threat that it will all wind up
As ground meat in a tin.

Ipouspoboba the veins

50. The Veins

What if it all blows up?
Absentmindedly they told me,
Oh, just do the veins
And stop complaining.
Do the veins? As if someone said,
Take out the garbage,
Or sweep the carpenter's shop.
It's not just the different layers
In every vein wall; has anyone
Ever counted the spider micro-veins
In just one average nose?
Place one of these creatures
Into the cold, what happens?
The toes, the fingers, the noses
Fall off! Just do the veins,
They said. Have someone
Standing in one place for a long time,
What happens? The veins turn varicose.
All they have to do
Is overeat, and what happens?
Heart failure, high blood pressure,
Stroke, diabetes, cancer, osteoarthritis,
Gallstones, infertility!
You create life, and it slips
Out of your hand and away,
Develops its own life, its own mind,
Which mostly amounts to mindlessness,

And you watch incredulously,
Wondering what happened
To all the care invested,
To even the smallest realization
That a body is a gift
To be accepted in gratitude,
To be held in some sort of esteem.
Quite the contrary,
There is a defiance in these creatures,
A subversive disregard, almost
Like a determination to terminate life
As soon as possible and at any cost.

Bineborin the arteries

51. The Arteries

Oh yea, cool! The Arteries!
Make it flow, the blood,
Make it pump all over,
Thump, thump, thump,
To the heart, yea,
Paint with the big brush,
With the impressionist brush,
The broad swath gushing,
Hot blood lava, raptures of outpouring,
The back and forth of surge and gush,
The carrying and retrieving,
Eternal trade in oxygen
To clients remote or impending.
As long as it trickles and glides
We welcome tomorrow
In the hush of morning's river.
It's murmuring, unheard,
Until something triggers awareness
And a roaring is in the ears.
Who can rob you

Of the red ambrosia?
Stay away from the insane mercenaries!
From warlocks,
Disguised as nighttime bats,
Looking for intoxicating swill!
You lift your pulsating hands
To joy, you raise your knees
In a victorious race,
You take in the opiate essence,
Found everywhere on earth,
You inhale it, snuff it in,
Chew on it, inject it
Into the amaranthine stream.
It carries euphoria
Into the fingertips, your eyes
Pour out the median dreams,
Your mouth winds a belt of words
Around your body, a torso stands
Silently in midair, high as a hawk's
Narrow wing, like, wasted.

Aatoimenpsephei the breaths in all the limbs

52. The Breath in All the Limbs

But that's what we've been
Talking about all along,
The breath-carrying blood,
The wave in every beat, bodily ebb and flow,
My happily high brother
Bineborin, making the highway,
My own measure and accordance
Filling it with life's traffic.
Our truth hidden from those who bear it
Out in the open. It is all part of nature's
Generosity, freely given and kept underway,
The lift of an arm, the kick of a leg,

The toss of a head,
Fueled by infinities of microscopic
Supply; without it, no eye has ever seen the grass,
No ear has heard a lover's exertion, no tongue tasted
A strawberry of spring, no brain concocted a plan
Or couched a phrase. It is always there,
The juice that goads, the adrenaline
That incites when the tiger growls,
The endorphin that floods
Every network at the touch of a hand.
This is not like walking
Out of an ambition,
Leaving behind a thought,
Or a word trailing your walk
Like a vanishing spoor.
We are always there, in the background,
Hidden in the deep layers
Of obscurity. We have resisted
All the poking of scientific
Research. The forms
That you have tried to impress
On the shapelessness of spirit,
Of uncanny agreements between
Mind and body, have all
Evaporated! How can you think
That you will ever have the vision
To extrapolate to the universal
From a gluon that doesn't really exist?

Entholleia all the flesh

53. All the Flesh

They are conspiring against the flesh!
Those two, Bineborin and Aatoimenpsephei,
Liberal loafers and layabouts!

We believe in the autonomy
Of every limb, we believe in the local right
Of self-determination! Do they really think
That the flesh is weak and the spirit
Willing? Whoever heard of such an
Upside-down world? Here you have
Two spaced-out lummoxes furling
The two main sails, and the flesh
Has no business endorsing either one.
We believe in every limb and every organ
Pursuing its own good in its own way,
So long as they do not attempt
To deprive any other limbs of theirs.
We have no wish to dominate; left to themselves,
The free flow of energy will bring freedom
Of operation to all segments of this body,
Trickling down into the minutest muscle.
This active participation, this civic virtue
Has always been an intrinsically valuable
Component of human flourishing,
Our emphatic commitment to administrative
Liberty. We will not tolerate any collapse
Into liberalism. If a limb wishes to be strong,
It needs to exercise. If the body wishes to run,
It needs to feed itself responsibly. Any limb
Neglecting itself will only earn what it deserves.
We have a rule of law, gentlemen!
Commit a crime against this human body,
And you may expect to be punished!
We have our yellow pencils at the ready,
Marking down all acts of conspiracy.
They have no business except to flow,
And not to make simplistic evaluations.
If there is a suspicion of scandal in that camp,
We will seek punishment for the culprits,
Even at the risk of bodily breakdown.

Bedouk the right buttock

54. The Right Buttock

Ribald the buttock and bun of Bedouk!
Let no one doubt this an erogenous zone,
Meant to excite devotees
Of either sex, and not to pay heed
To the drone and dismal jaw
Of flesh producers! Write thank you
Letters to Bedouk, who gave you
The right fanny, the tush, the gluteus,
The rump, the butt, the keister,
The derrière! Oh, madam,
What scandals we have in store
For you! Lead off your recalcitrant
Lovers with buttocks exposed,
Pay no attention to their cloven
Hooves. Thus were the Egyptian
Prisoners humbled by Assyria
And Ishmael called the ass
Of a man. Much better are
The nudes of Lautrec and Renoir,
The sculptures of Canova and Rodin.
Take yourself to the beach;
Find the traces of buttocks in the sand.
How ephemeral this evidence,
Not in clay, and nowhere permanent.
It must be a sculpture in your mind,
Erected within strains of thought,
Woven into the keys that bring you music,
Touched by the breath that bends the frame,
Blows away your deficiencies,
Impels you forward to new perspectives,
Obliges you to return and linger,
Celebrating what gives you resilience.
A gentle trace where the dimples
Are lightly shadowed. It will never leave you,

The warmth of this body,
Your words will be clumsy in recall,
Because you will refract each other's
Salacious thoughts and innuendos,
Your cheeks at both ends,
Rosy in blush—what smutty fun!

Arabeei the left buttock

55. The Left Buttock

Thinking this would be difficult,
I braced for the agonistic games,
The placement of every vein
Within its context of bulging material.
No sooner had I begun,
Than the mad Bedouk
Waved his wand of indelicacy
At the right side of this torso,
And all an angel had to do
Was direct the flow, catch the boundaries,
And allow them to run smoothly
To their natural end. It was,
After all, a zone of seductiveness.
My hands, not needing to refract,
Were all but idle. I provided the bed
That the river needed to gallop
Down the river. The brightest mind
Among the toiling assemblers
Remained hidden behind the scene-
Shifters and painters, knowing
That such passion and foolishness
Would only come to grief.
Come, take my keys,
I offer you this torrent
To sweep you down-slope.
To externalize, like the mad Bedouk.

There are sluts of either sex, willing to challenge
Anyone at the beach or in the tavern.
There are self-effacing dreamers,
Hot within, cool without, always
Bashful, never showing their frantic
Desires. Be casual, is my motto,
Because the placid rivers
Do not tear away their own banks.
The ransom is a smiling sun,
Able to reflect in a smoother veneer.
Sitzfleisch is better used for study
Than for acts of lechery.

...the penis

56. The Penis

Iconoclasm wiped the name
Of this contrary *propria persona.*
Placed in a box according to size,
The penis would be domiciled
At the piffling end of the roster.
No ballast for the buttocks, an orphan,
Singly pointing at the great world,
And mostly homeless.
The right hand of the infant found it there,
In the crotch, and would always locate
The same route for leakage and for fun.
Stern-faced ecclesiastics assiduously
Eyeballed the accessory, pronouncing it
Toxic to moral actuality, a curse
To procreation, a clear outline for all
Invented sin. Better tuned out than tugged. I sing
The ejaculatory rapture, the popping
Of the pod, the spreading of pollen among
Tenderhearted flowers of spring, to spite

The priggish sermonizers. I eulogize
Insertion into agreeable apertures,
The Flying Cloud under full sail.
When does the infant recognize itself?
This is where existential gold is raked
Instead of money. Do you want to chase it,
Like a chicken that's flown the coop?
It will play dead when you need it most,
Or it won't play dead. It will shoot straight,
And back your way on the rebound,
Winging sons and daughters into your face.
Also good for pissing contests, if you know
How to sight the azimuth of intention.
Beware a thinking penis! It will never
Assert itself when the breach is won.
Self-consciously it will temporize about
Mind-body coordination and what should be
Its grand design for maximum attainment.
By the time a strategy has been decided
The day is gone and so is half the team.

Eilo the testicles

57. The Testicles

Manufacturing something
That manufactures something
Else, we will be the dynamo
Within the dynamo, the alma mater
Of all things mammalian.
The two dangling fruits,
Expanding, contracting in
Temperature extremes.
This black forest of hair is useless,
Hides nothing that can be seen.
Poor twins that work and cooperate,

But never inside, where the fun
Takes place. Did I say, they need
Protection? Not made of iron,
But so soft, we thought we had
Created a creature that would not be
Able to sit or cross its legs.
Venerable men, holding forth about
The phenomenology of truth, while
Their two nuts were swinging back
And forth. No wonder the male side
Chose to hide behind its dungarees
And pantaloons. Hide something
And it will eventually attain to
A symbolic eminence. This
Was a joke of the higher divinities:
Attach a swinging add-on
Where it would be most vulnerable.
Our nuts are shriveling, our dynamos
Refuse to mass-produce the pollen
That used to float freely through the air,
And nature is unwilling to be as wasteful
As she used to be. One thing we have not
Discussed among this group of pioneers:
All of it happens in time. What will time do
When it passes lazily through its millions,
All of the swinging cojones slowly begin
To dry up, the pollen ceases to flow,
And this torso we've been working on
So meticulously ceases to have offspring?

Sorma the genitals

58. The Genitals

Excuse me? Did we not
Just belabor penis and testicles?
Does one plus one equal three? No prairie oysters

In your prairie? Did the wind change
Suddenly and sweep you off
Your denotation? Sorma wanders
In the streets of Memphis, searching
For the characteristic shape of my Lord's
Throbbing metaphor. My Lord, the King,
Has the attention span of a gnat.
A nanny attends him at all times,
Pene statuettes litter the place
From floor to roof. What fun
The archaeologists will have when they
Find the tangible icons
Of his depravity. The phallus of Childe
Horus measures twice the girth
And three times the height of his entire
Body. On the other hand, my Lord,
The King, has a pud the size of an Athenian
Tetradrachm. This has in no wise
Diminished the size of his ego. All
Artistic portrayals show him enormously
Erect. The Nile floods at its rising, the Nubian enemy
Flees in horror, and the entire harem
Swoons. He flings his semen left and right, brandishing
The hose like an elephant blasting
Dust all over his body. Anyone whose
Eyes take in this spectacle is turned
To stone, precisely as if looking at
Medea. The phallus moves back and forth,
Like a piston in oiled chambers,
Suffering pangs of piston envy, because
My piston is not your piston, and I
Have written mine as a wand of love.
If you close your mouth, you can still
Taste the oil, provided your eyes happen
Not to be hereditary, and blink in their own
Lubricant. Never quail before the obligatory
Blast into brilliantly different bridleways.

59. The Right Thigh

The right thigh is the thigh
Of ages. When you lift this thigh,
You will know that you are dealing
With quality. Let's talk about this
For ten seconds. Any longer,
And I get bored. So don't interrupt
Anything I say, and remove that
Handicapped person from the audience.
Any time you want to deal,
All you have to do is come to my tower.
But don't use the left stairway.
That's mine, and it's private.
Don't mind the guys standing down there,
By the main entrance, wearing swastikas.
They're my personal guards. They're here
To make sure that the construction
Of this right thigh moves forward
In a deliberate, steady, conservative
Manner. Some of these limbs
Will have to be dismantled, mark my words!
What was I saying? Get that right thigh
In here! If these people bother you,
Push them out of the way! What are they doing here?
If you kick them in the butt, they'll
Thank you for it. Boy, look at that one,
What I wouldn't do to her! They love it
You know. All they need to see is,
That you're in charge, that you're the alpha,
And they'll melt right in your hand.
Listen, I can't stay here all day.
Kick that guy with the clip-board and the pen.
What's he doing here? Is he supposed to check
Up on us? There's nothing for you to do here.
Go back behind your borders, go back

Behind the wall where you belong!
It's getting too hot around here.
Just get on with it. I'm going to have
Myself a snack and a snooze.
That thing better be in place
When I get back, unless you want
To deal with my goons.

Nebrith the left thigh

60. The Left Thigh

That's right. Get that femur over here.
Snap it into the hip. And don't you think
That my attitude is in your favor,
Or that our thoughts are alike. I'm with
Gormakaiochlabar, we don't take guff
From anybody. What happens to the rest
Of this body is up to the other morons.
I see those goons down there, what
Do you think? They guard our crew
As much as anyone's. Nazi goons at the pearly
Gates! They keep things as mellow
As a whore under the night-lights of Pigalle.
I know it's hard work, I do, really, and here
I am, I'm your voice to the man upstairs,
Everyone included. When you've done
Your job it'll be great, you'll see, I promise you.
If we can keep those liberals from screwing
Up the limbs, this guy will be a rock star.
He'll be stomping the boards and wowing
The groupies. This will be a new act,
A language of the common people, it'll be tuned
To all the right amps, and they'll write about it
Until the pens go out of style. What's happening
Down there? What are you wrapping around,
Like, the ass? What's it called? The Gluteus

Maximus? I hope you know what you're doing,
Because I won't be held responsible.
It's not our job, anyway, we're here to produce
The base for your guys, but I'm telling you,
I'm not inviting you to any of my parties.
Alright crew, I think we're done here,
Let's go have a brew on the house.
You want to stay and watch? What are you watching?
You just installed the bones, so you know
Bones. You saw how the other morons
Wrapped the ass, so you know what meat
Looks like. What more do you need?
The veins, the arteries, the blood, the blah,
You're kidding me, right? Go ahead, stay.
All of you just got on my wrong side,
And this interview is over!

Pserem the muscles of the right leg

61. The Muscles of the Right Leg

Pserem figured he had the right
To manufacture the right leg,
But had not counted on the power
Of the shop union. Pandemonium
Among seraphic proletarians.
Those under Ormaoth, that greedy
Self-seeker, would not allow anyone
To touch the armature until it was
Unconditionally finished, attached,
And aching for the muscles, aching
For the hamstrings, quadriceps,
And the tendon of Achilles.
The flesh began screaming in agony,
Lodging traumatic memory
In its construction, a precursor

Of cramps and seizures in subsequent
Strains and efforts. It was,
After all, a potential weapon,
Able to kick footballs of various
Shapes and sizes, the neighbor's
Shins, or the robber's nuts. Take heed, lawmen:
Mass-murderers are created
By shoddily shod individuals!
These were not made *ex nihilo*,
They were brought together out of
Chaos, which attained to glory
And self-recognition when their
Atoms jumped all their traces,
Puck-puck-puck, and aligned themselves
Into a sexually attractive limb,
Remembering forever the loathsome
Skulk and funk of inauguration,
When chaos was organized into
Resplendent fractals, when foot soles
Found a thousand ways of being
Numb, sensitive, callused, hard
As nails to the point of walking
On live coals. But since when
Do insubordinate seraphim
Need health insurance?

Asaklas the muscles of the left leg

62. The Muscles of the Left Leg

None of this has been happening
With the classic furniture of *mise*
En scene or stage direction. We
Are hearing loud voices arguing
Over who bears responsibility for
Building and fitting one thing into

Another. They'll be infesting some
Minor planet in a galaxy,
A suburb of the All. Don't ever
Believe in this ubiquitous noise; one angel's
Finger disturbing the divine magnetic
Field is all it takes. The field yields
Endless creatures and palaces,
Peopled with convoluted times
Running amok, berserk mineral
Matter devoid of gravity, not knowing
Where to exist. These proceedings
Should be happening quietly,
With dignity, without tumult.
Instead, we infuse this universe
With imperfection and hostility,
As if they were a *sine qua non*.
In order to complete this humble task,
I came here artlessly, expecting
To enter, do the work, and leave.
What is this screaming flesh?
Incredibly, these divine messengers
Came to make of charity
A lonely orphan, of quiet occupation
A raucous malingerer bent on payment.
I will this limb unconscious consciousness,
An infusion of my angelic essence,
These unassuming brawny fibers
Discharging their function effortlessly,
Like a healing wound. I imagine
Them occupied in walks through woods,
Climbing ladders, balancing on roofs,
And slowly wilting through their century,
Until they become dust again,
Like a line drawing in the sand.

Ormaoth the right leg

63. The Right Leg

A tremendous responsibility!
It's like building the continent of Italy
Into the Mediterranean storms!
I charge all of you with my own
Stern gravitas to keep the other angel
Resources out of the way, until
Every last fragment of the armature
Has been assembled! You there,
Get that heel in place! Untangle those veins
And get them enfolded into the muscle!
Ho, Pserem! Move your personnel
Out of our way, and stay clear of the thigh!
That idiot, I won't pronounce his name,
Is liable to ruin everything with his short,
(Or nonexistent), attention span. I swear,
Do any of you even know
What is happening up north? Have you
Ever heard of a hip, or a shoulder blade?
Have you heard what Phnouth did
To the left hip, and the shock that
Reverberated through this entire continent?
Of course you haven't, you were too
Busy plying each other with your witty epigrams.
Well, here's my overture to you:
We are building what will be
The most destructive creature
Ever assembled by our natural causes.
This human will kill everything
That moves, not because he needs to,
But for sport. He will cleverly invent
Millions of objects for his own comfort,
And then drown his planet with garbage
As soon as he's finished with them.

He will scream and yell about things
Of which he knows nothing, and he will be
A mass-murderer and cannibal, not just
Of strangers, but of his own family. And that, my friends,
Is what you are helping to create. Welcome to reality!
Let's paste and powder and grow and glue
This lousy son of a bitch!

Emenun the left leg

64. The Left Leg

We have poured a libation
Of blood for this left leg.
Long may it propel forward
The one who bears it; may it stem
The heave of a heavy oar,
The sway of a footrope
Under a main upper topgallant sail.
This leg will go places
Where we cannot follow,
And when it comes back
We will not be here for welcome.
Our faces will be a taciturn
Mirror in the blood of the offspring.
How will this creature remember its own truth?
It will go astray and forget
How the original composition
Was brought about. When you
Drink of yourself daily, there is no
Recognition of taste, but the bland dryness
That devours all other savors.
This will be a model for the *Discobolus* of Myron,
For Michelangelo's *David*,
The flesh and stone will breathe
More ardently when examined

By children and scholars.
The children will tiptoe through mud
And leave behind delicate spoors,
And sacrificial blood will flow
When they step into thorns.
It will be the beginning of their return,
The first red drops to be absorbed
Back into the dust from whence
They came. See the fresh lips,
Torn by pain and laughter!
Our hands at the keys produce this music,
Which is life. How we are racked
By the doubt of our own possibility,
Disbelieving in our own sound and flesh,
As though we were speaking Akkadian
To a homeless person in Detroit!

Knux the right shin

65. The Right Shin

Make that tibia as strong
As a major bone should be!
If you take a look at the right thigh,
You will know that it was made
Of shoddy particulars, and
The entire phallus is beneath
Contempt! There will be humans
Who never experience anything,
And there will be others who
Will stumble from one emergency
To another. Any truthful answer will defy
Expression, but this bone
Will survive the centuries
In its tomb, eventually to come
To rest on a laboratory shelf,

Measured and weighed by near-sighted
Interns. You have given the universe
A form, buried in layered buildup,
The concluding metaphor of life.
This dangerous organism will strive
To understand itself, willing to risk
Life and leg just to know anything at all!
It will probe the deficiencies with stubborn
Dedication, and will seek to self correct
What you have fouled up, and it may even
Determine who is at fault! In dissolute
Nights it will bellow about the drunken
Divine cherubic godfathers who set about
To work on its carcass and infused
The entire anatomy with nothing but
Poisons! Luckily, the majority
Of these creatures will be comatose
Most of the time, and the least aware
Of all limbs will be the shin, the Olympian
Enduring facet you are trying to shave
Into shape with your clumsy hands.
Things that are valid usually have no mouth
To holler gibberish, and no ears to hear
Political flapdoodle, and no senses
To feel the onslaught of decadence.

Tupelon the left shin

66. The Left Shin

While we were trying to work
On this shin, there was an outside
Breach into the organization!
Who was the mole? Privately
We suspect some of the lackeys

Among the northern lunatics. I felt
That we would land wherever
A human consciousness dared
An attempt at comprehending
This project, and us into the bargain.
Following the trail, we happened
Upon the 21st century, where an old
Self-important halfwit, living
In a Milwaukee hellhole, had embarked
Upon the deplorable ambition
To reconstruct an angelic history
About the creation of Adam.
According to his own pathetic
Reconstruction, he is, at this very moment,
Writing about the left shin!
From now on, our existence will consist
In blocking his progress, to stand in the way
Of what he believes he has achieved!
We will unleash demons to feast
On his brain, and sirens to turn him
Into a fruitcake! Blow his fuses!
Kill all of his lights! Give him a plague
Of cockroaches! Trash his appliances,
Remove all of the markets from his neighborhood!
Afflict him with petty diseases! Pester him
With impossible neighbors! Break
His windows in the middle of winter!
We will give him a left shin to write about!
Who does he think he is? Do his friends
And relatives even believe that he is still
Of sound mind? Should he not be hidden from the public
To avoid the embarrassment of these
Senile stabs at notoriety,
With the delusional intent of taking down
The pyramids of Egypt?

Achiel the right ankle

67. The Right Ankle

There, there, right ankle,
When we are finished with you,
You will have learned what are
The first steps toward falling
In love. Poor thing, with so many
Parts, what are your chances
Of avoiding a sprain? We will
Carefully, lovingly, place each part,
Because we adore you; we will hover
About as you jump from one
Puddle to the next or clear a high fence.
We will always be there to heal
The breaks. Move this way, move
That way, it all coheres; it all
Obeys your volition. A miracle
Of convergences, bearing the vertical
Posture of the entire body!
Nothing univocal about this, a choir
Of bone, singing in astonishing
Harmony! Follow now, follow
The baton of the maestro,
As you hop, skip, and jump
From one lack of thought to
Another. No reason to pay heed,
The thing works magnificently without
The slightest additional exertion.
The calcaneus, oh, the calcaneus,
Was there ever a more magnificent
Bone? We were unable to give you the wings
Of Hermes; you will be earthbound,
Enduring the heavy pull of *Terra Mater*
Who loves you too much, requiring of herself
A clinging disposition. How could she

Avoid being stricken with adoration
For such a beauteous attribute?
This work of art, so embedded in its
Function, unable to respond to anything
Except the hard surface of a courtyard,
Gambling its form mindlessly
At every skip and frolic!

Phneme the left ankle

68. The Left Ankle

Look at him: Achiel,
"The Brother of God."
He actually thinks that he
Deserves this title. All of them,
Oblivious that the omniscient
Newscaster has given us report
Of unseemly happenings.
That crowd renders angels
A standard template for imbeciles,
And Adam more intelligent
Than all who labored at his mediocrity.
We're working quietly, competently, like Archimedes,
Levering one attitude with another,
Attempting to make light of all the botched universals.
If there was any decency in any of these chiselers,
They would cease and desist
From even the smallest try
At anything! If someone shouted
Fire! And this body began burning
At the head, those at the shoulders
Would be oblivious, the artisans
Of the neck would hum and hone
Until the fire crawled up their keister!
And if the fire does not get him,

He will be shot like a buffalo,
And all his companions will sniffle
At the grass uneasily, knowing that
Something may have gone amiss,
But unable to explain why Adam is not moving anymore.
And after the uneasy sniffle,
Those who could not rescue him
Will grieve no more than is good
For their constitution. The choir
Will replace the lost tenor with two,
The orchestra its fallen drummer
With the entire percussive mob,
Unless he was lucky enough
To have a partner who moved
Through his anima
Like a torrent of holy water.

Phiouthrom the right foot

69. The Right Foot

Can't get much further south
Than this. Are you asking this foot to wander
Where the earth is shaking,
Where everyone is in denial
About the toppling houses all around?
Don't ask the wind to bind this foot
To the fiery glass walk on a tropical island.
Next to the tent they stomped a debkah
Into the dusty surface, a line of men
Reaching down to the Wadi,
Hands clapping, with wailing shepherd's flute,
Chest and hip so close to the next,
You couldn't force a dagger in between.
Glue to avoid the drifting angel feathers
Loosened in the wake of blasphemy.

In the rain you smash into walls,
The bricks quiver in spicy mortar.
Bending knee at one-and-a-half,
Right foot forward, reach over the bronze plate,
Rice and veal doused in olive oil;
Don't cry for the victims of our last feud.
They are in Paradise with their seventy virgins,
And all their hands were empty when they departed.
Let the wind sweep on its own,
Carrying away the smoke of incineration.
Give it your gestures, not your blasphemies.
This foot will not know where to go,
Having always the feeling of arrival,
Of no need to wander into wildness;
Like a goat seeking green and wet,
It needs a shepherd to make choices.
You see a radiant face, spectacular body, long slim hands,
Strong hands to pound Liszt into compliance,
Legs to make a misogynist swoon,
And the shock of a bony foot.
This was never the limb of a goddess,
No matter the rouge on toenails,
Not helped by all the bars in Phoenix,
Nor magnified by infrared light.

Boabel its toes

70. The Toes of the Right Foot

This little piggy went to attend a meeting
Of nail-clippers anonymous. This little piggy
Preferred to be what they forbade
Cruella to be. This little piggy ate spoons of pepper
And went to the back seat to cry.
This little piggy avoided all spices
And became an insufferably wholesome

Maverick. And this little piggy yelled
When all the other piggies got stubbed
In a stone field and scared
The hell out of an amphora toe.
Would God love His toe-creature?
Would God cringe if it took them out
With a crossbow? Does God ever cringe?
I solemnly promise to defend toe after toe,
Forward movement, or lack of endowment.
In toe heaven there will never be
The desperation of athlete's foot,
A tenfold joy. Very long ago
These things were fins, in case you feel like
An iron-capped kick in the aristocratic butt.
Standing toe to toe, with a different
Indifference. Legislation of foot-massagers.
All these hinges, segments, linkages,
Stubbed fields of pain, self-tethered
Clumsy ticks of movement, damp worms
Hibernating in rotten shrouds. Whiffs like
Humid summer lightning, shooting out from
Rotten socks. Black mold
Like fireworks in veins, biting with a hundred
Stingers. A powder bath tonight,
Before these toes mingle with someone else's,
Little kicks under linen. Where toes begin,
A sententious anatomy as bland as a sandwich
Suddenly begins to know what to do.
Worse things have happened in a fermenting
Fish barrel. Drink up and be emptied,
Via rivers in which the sticklebacks
Can nibble all the accumulations of your life.

Trachoun the left foot

71. The Left Foot

If you haven't apprehended yet
What exactly we do, here it is:
There are thoughts flying around
The entire universe, since the universe
Is composed of thought. It has fallen
To me, Trachoun, to ferret out
And catch every thought pertaining
To a left foot, no matter where
It is hiding, like a much-too-clever
Termite. I descend down deep
To the eternal key, the universal
"Let there be," and place it into the lock,
The conceptualized prototype of all
Feet. This happens in a consciousness
That is not conscious, but is focused on the billions
Of electrons shaping one thought,
"Left Foot," and transcending the conscious
Thought itself, which through several levels
Of transcendence forms those very
Thought electrons into a physical reality,
Into a left foot. Humans could be walking through palaces
Fulfilling their most irrational dreams.
They know intuitively that their role gets lost.
Someone steps on a left foot,
There is the obligation to scream, to derail the self
Into a syntax of self-conscious
Self-justifications, a hail-covered
Field of crosses, where silent serenity
Has been crucified. Obligation
To be distracted by deliberate noise,
To drown out everything, including

The intimate recognition of love,
The silence that would terrorize a jittery mind.
No chance of ever creating a left foot out of nothing.
This legacy of thoughts and words,
Kept in cabinets like a dowry. Who will be the lucky bride,
The recipient of all this precious claptrap?
Billions of humans have relaxed next to security's fireplace,
Warming their oblivious left feet.

Phikna its toes

72. The Toes of the Left Foot

Why bust your head
Over something inconsequential?
These toes, abstracted upon a left foot,
Are uniquely *our* undertaking. When did *you* last
Check on the holy shekel He gave you?
This is our chapter, which followed us
And clung to our robes as we ambled
Through the sand dunes. Who can tell
Why it chose us, who were humble
Wanderers through the heartbroken
Morning shadows. The demand came
Upon us like a flow of lava, liquid fire.
Had we refused, our eyes would never
Have stopped watching; the gavel in our hands
Would have pounded the validation
Of our judgment forever. Our creature
Began to stumble about, as though
There was something to be gained
Beyond the natural hedges. Why did it stray
Out of the tropics and into the frost?
Did it not feel the signs of trespassing
Upon the unsettled pathway? But then,
It was not. The teeth came out of the ground,

The thorns on the citrus trees were enormous,
The torso wrapped itself in double and triple
Layers of skin, pulled tight the rope that bound
And fettered every limb, dreamed
Of being jammed into a fur prison
That had dissolved in one of the snowmelts
Of ghostly Eden. Hairy Neanderthals,
Scaling the icebergs, gave themselves wholly
To the sharp-edged game of survival.
We had to adapt to multiple Adams
Who crowded the heaven-bound float
And threatened to capsize our accomplishment.
Where are the feet and soles and toes
We created, which should have danced
Through their own immortality
Like ten ballet pinkies on a hippo?

Miamai the toenails

73. The Toenails

We had to file them down;
They were spiritual talons.
He wanted to claw everything
Alive, until we got him domesticated.
What you've forgotten, the savage
Legacy resting in the deepest lakes,
Is what influences you most.
This man was the wildest thing
We had ever seen. He was already obsolete before
We finished him. The toenails wiggled
Crazily when we hammered them in,
As if tons of stress were trying to pour
Out of them and into a sinister rendezvous
With bad behavior. Like pushover parents,
We coddled him and tried to keep him

Lassoed to the garden gate. Sometimes
He sat there laughing, and tried
To whisper twelve tribes in cotes
Of dove, but only crows came out.
They perched on his shoulders as if
Condemned, and all the time living within
The breath of Adam's whisper, when he himself
Was only a whisper, because his actual torso
Was down there, comatose as yet, in Eden.
The keratin resisted for eons, the weavers
Wove and wove to set the inner spines.
This is the difficulty, when angels try
To fabricate the base and grieving bits
Of common matter, strange declarations
Ooze from the electronic juice that supposedly
Holds it all together. Cooperation of the createe
At the lowest low, unwilling in the whole
Process, disinclined to be in the world,
Thank you very much! And every electron
Needing a special invitation to go
Where it was needed, to do what an electron
Was supposed to do, but communicating
Its intractability with ten thousand flourishes!
But how, in the name of the Almighty,
Did all of this register in a lousy toenail?

Labernioum…

74. …

I'm talking to you now, you, who did these "deeds."
If you want my opinion, scrap the whole thing
And start from scratch! Liberal dimwits,
Trying to create transcendent qualities in soft matter,
Botching the formula at every step!

Gangsters, threatening their own creation!
Conservative racists bent
On sabotaging work intrinsic to their own!
This man, Adam, is at war with himself, because
Of you! Every limb is at war
With every other limb! This work
Of yours has made you experts at uselessness!
No one has ever been more guilty than you!
…
        Yes, yes, here I am,
Gabriel. How may I serve you?
Desist? How am I to desist,
When every shoddy thing I see
Offends my moral faculties?
…
You're kidding me!
…
No, I do not, Gabriel, want to
Second-guess the Almighty,
But you will have to explain to me
This carnage, which I find
Deeply offensive and upsetting.
…
Oh, I see, I see, hm—, hm—.
So he was made in God's image.
…
Hm—, in the image of God.
Was he *really* made in the image of God?
…
I'm trying to answer you,
But there is nothing I can say.
Nothing at all. Who would dare
To contest the Almighty?
…
Oh dear.
Oh dear.

Notes

Creation of the Left Eye: Does the moon really have a bald eye: From the poem *Straw Hat*. Cf. Rita Dove, 2016:119, *Collected Poems: 1974-2004*.

Creation of the Molars: King Harald's toothache: Cf. 1954, Frans G. Bengtsson, *The Long Ships*, (translated from the Swedish by Michael Meyer).

Creation of the Throat: their throat is an open sepulcher; Psalms 5:9.

Creation of the Right Hand: "Something has spoken to me in the night," from Thomas Wolfe's *You Can't Go Home Again*.

Creation of the Fingers of the Right Hand: Those icy fingers up and down my spine, from *That Old Black Magic,* Songwriters Johnny Mercer and Harold Arlen. The air, the air is everywhere! *Air Lyrics* (From *Hair*), Songwriters James Rado, Gerome Ragni, Galt Mac Dermot.

Creation of the Fingers of the Left Hand: "And he shall set the sheep on his right, but the goats on his left." Matthew 25:33.

About FutureCycle Press

FutureCycle Press is dedicated to publishing exceptional English-language poetry books, chapbooks, and anthologies in both print-on-demand and Kindle ebook formats. Founded in 2007 by long-time independent editor/publishers and partners Diane Kistner and Robert S. King, the press incorporated as a nonprofit in 2012. A number of our editors are distinguished poets and writers in their own right, and we have been actively involved in the small press movement going back to the early seventies.

The FutureCycle Poetry Book Prize and honorarium is awarded annually for the best full-length volume of poetry we publish in a calendar year. Introduced in 2013, our Good Works projects are anthologies devoted to issues of universal significance, with all proceeds donated to a related worthy cause. Our Selected Poems series highlights contemporary poets with a substantial body of work to their credit; with this series we strive to resurrect work that has had limited distribution and is now out of print.

We are dedicated to giving all of the authors we publish the care their work deserves, making our catalog of titles the most diverse and distinguished it can be, and paying forward any earnings to fund more great books.

We've learned a few things about independent publishing over the years. We've also evolved a unique, resilient publishing model that allows us to focus mainly on vetting and preserving for posterity poetry collections of exceptional quality without becoming overwhelmed with bookkeeping and mailing, fundraising activities, or taxing editorial and production "bubbles." To find out more about what we are doing, come see us at www.futurecycle.org.

The FutureCycle Poetry Book Prize

All full-length volumes of poetry published by FutureCycle Press in a given calendar year are considered for the annual FutureCycle Poetry Book Prize. This allows us to consider each submission on its own merits, outside of the context of a contest. Too, the judges see the finished book, which will have benefitted from the beautiful book design and strong editorial gloss we are famous for.

The book ranked the best in judging is announced as the prize-winner in the subsequent year. There is no fixed monetary award; instead, the winning poet receives an honorarium of 20% of the total net royalties from all poetry books and chapbooks the press sold online in the year the winning book was published. The winner is also accorded the honor of being on the panel of judges for the next year's competition; all judges receive copies of all contending books to keep for their personal library.

Made in the USA
Columbia, SC
04 April 2018